THE BATTLE OF THE WOMBS

AND THE THIRD FORCE THAT FUELS IT

The Battle of the Wombs

Copyright © 2020 Osien Sibanda

The author has asserted his right to be identified as the author of this work in accordance with the Copyright, Designs and Patents Act 1988. All rights reserved. No part of this publication may be reproduced, stored in a retrieval system, or transmitted, in any form or by any means, electronic, mechanical, photocopying, recording or otherwise without the prior permission of Sibanda Publishing.

All Scripture quotations, unless otherwise indicated, are taken from the Holy Bible, New International Version, UK edition, copyright © 1973, 1978, 1984 by International Bible Society. Published by Hodder and Stoughton. Used by permission. All rights reserved.

Scripture quotations marked NKJV are taken from the Holy Bible, New King James Version®, copyright © 1982 by Thomas Nelson, Inc. Used by permission.

All rights reserved.

Scripture quotations marked KJV are taken from the Holy Bible, King James Version, Cambridge University Press, Oxford University Press, HarperCollins and the Queen's Printers.

Scripture quotations marked GNT are taken from the Holy Bible, Good News Translation Version, Copyright © 1992 American Bible Society. All rights reserved.

Scripture quotations marked NLT are taken from the Holy Bible, New Living Translation, copyright 1996. Used by permission of Tyndale House Publishers, Inc., Wheaton, Illinois 60189. All rights reserved.

A catalogue record for this book is available from the British Library.

Published in the United Kingdom by Sibanda Publishing.

ISBN: 978-0-9935446-6-8

CONTENTS

Introduction 5

1 The Third Force 9

2 The Right Way 19

3 The Challenge 21

4 The Stronghold 25

5 The Battle of the Wombs 29

6 Is There a Model? 33

7 The Ideal Relationship 37

INTRODUCTION

The stories of challenges, fights, mistrust and tensions between a daughter-in-law and mother-in-law cut across classes, cultures and nations.

From the Middle East to Africa, from the Americas to Europe, Australia and China, the battles of a mother-in-law and daughter-in-law are similar. This suggests that there is a spiritual battle behind these conflicts, directed and choreographed by a common demon. Otherwise, how could these attitudes and practices be so alike across so many diverse families in such diverse homelands?

The goal of this demon, it appears, is to break the family and weaken society and trivialise the institution of marriage. With more people either fearing to commit to marriage or seeing no need for marriage today, many people in our society opt for co-habitation. In this looser arrangement, the couple can get involved without commitment, leading to many compromised homes and wounded children. The problem is that these wounded children do not remain children. One day they will grow up to be mothers and fathers who are wounded. And guess what? Wounded fathers wound children, wounded mothers wound children, wounded partners wound each other, and the pattern continues down through the generations.

Today prisons are full of men and women who trace their psychological and emotional wounds (and sometimes physical wounds!) to the problems in their family. I came across a number of young men who were in prison for murdering their own fathers because of how the fathers treated their mothers. Further investigations revealed the instability in the home where in-laws were involved. Because we do not see the hand of the enemy in these relationships, we tend to make mother-in- law and daughter-in-law jokes that we laugh about. Because we see them as jokes, we do not devote time and prayer to fix this problem. In the end, it goes on and on like a virus – harming society and future generations in the process. The fact that these dysfunctional relationships are so prevalent in society is shown by the frequency with which they are turned into comedy themes for stand-up comedians!

There is an Italian proverb that says, "Mother-in-law and daughter-in-law, storm and hail." Storm and hail speak of destruction and turmoil. If we are not careful, we begin to believe that this problem is just normality for these relationships, and allow this evil to fester. The French often say, "Mothers-in-law and daughters-in-law can be cooked together but they will never be tender." This proverb paints a difficult, almost impossible relationship. It creates a picture of something that does not work and will never work. The result is a society that is resistant to marriage, but because young people naturally want to be involved in a relationship, more and more of them resort to cohabitation.

This is the magnitude of the challenge we have created, because familiarity with the problem has desensitised us to the difficulties of this very important relationship. It is often presented as a one-sided argument that claims either the daughter-in-law or the mother-in-law is to blame. Because of this, no one takes responsibility, no one self-examines, no one thinks back to consider the seeds they are sowing.

The problem with seeds is that they grow and spread more seeds, eventually turning into a forest. It is sad to say that some mother-in-law and daughter-in-law relationships are now forests that require heavy machinery to clear if they are to find a good relationship with each other. There are daughters-in-law who are problematic and

INTRODUCTION

controlling, but the same can also be said about certain mothers-in-law. This is a typical sign of a wound and the approach would be to try and help resolve issues before it is too late. This could be done by promoting successful relationships and beginning to counter the negative narrative. Good role models could be encouraged to share their life stories to help people change their perceptions.

CHAPTER ONE

THE THIRD FORCE

Having listened and observed many of these mother/daughter-in-law battles play out, I have come to realise that the son plays an important role in fuelling or resolving this battle. He is the third force that is capable of neutralising misunderstanding and any overbearing by individuals who should not be involved in the marriage relationship, like his mother and his family.

The mother-in-law gets her power to interfere from her son each time he fails to protect his wife from his mother. This can occur when the son does not correct his mother in the presence of his wife each time his mother crosses the line in the marriage. This happens when the mother (first womb) and son (third force) have a very close relationship that is unhealthy for the marriage. An unhealthy relationship between a mother and son can easily filter into the son's marriage relationship with his wife (second womb), resulting in friction and insecurity among the three of them.

When a mother and son side with each other most of the time and make the wife feel like an outsider, the wife becomes the shortest side of the triangle – so to speak. What defines this unhealthy relationship? The mother-in-law is too attached to her son and ends up becoming a shadow over her son's marriage that is overbearing, pushing out the new wife. The son is so close to his mother that he is managed by her in all he does. Decisions for the marriage are filtered through his mother in order for them to be carried out. The mother becomes the second woman in the marriage, not in adulterous ways, of course, but certainly in a destructive way.

The mother-in-law wants the attention of both her husband and her son. This is selfishness and short-sightedness that is very damaging for her son's marriage. It stifles the confidence of the wife, leaving her choking on the over-involvement of her mother-in-law. The Greeks offer good advice for such a mother-in-law: "The grumbling mother in-law forgets that she was once a bride."

It is at this point that the man must step in and put his mother in her place: close to her own husband. The son must be courageous enough to tell his mother to mind her own home. Unfortunately, men often fail to ask their mothers to disassociate themselves from the affairs of their homes, because they think it is dishonouring to do so. In most African cultures for instance, it is considered dishonour to rebuke your mother. And of course, the Bible tells us to honour our parents, so for Christian Africans the problem can be exacerbated. But it is not dishonouring your mother to tell her that her advice is welcome but you are not necessarily going to follow it. A couple must make their own decisions otherwise they have not truly become adults.

As a result of the false idea that honouring the mother has to include obeying her, even when the man has become an adult, many mothers get away with it and continue to harm the marriage in the process. When a man listens to his mother more than he does his wife, he fuels this battle and gives more ammunition to his mother. This results in the daughter-in-law beginning a battle to eliminate her mother-in-law from her space. The mother in-law in turn may begin to think the daughter in-law does not like her. She can communicate this to the son and before long, unholy alliances form. This can become complicated if the man sides with his mother. If the matter is not resolved quickly, a lot of harm can occur within relationships and families, as is illustrated in the different proverbs across the world.

The Bible laid the foundation for marriage that limits this friction in **GENESIS 2:24**: *"A man leaves his father and mother and is united to his* *wife, and they become one flesh."* A man has never truly left his parents if he is more united to his mother than his wife. For a new marriage to be successful, the man must leave his family attachments that he has been so used to. He must leave his father and his mother and form a new bond of attachment with his wife. Jesus alluded to this important principle in **MATTHEW 19:6**: *"So they are no longer two, but one flesh."*

Most marriages do not get to this stage of oneness because they do not follow the principle. It is very easy to be separated by other people if you are not fully joined to each other, and the facilitator of this joining is the man, which is why the wife takes on his name. We must help our wives connect with us into that oneness.

The last part of **MATTHEW 19:6** says: *"Therefore what God has joined together, let no one separate."* The first man to allow that separation is the son, by his failure to leave his mother, father, and the rest of his family! He also allows that separation by failing to pull his wife to his side and work together with her. The siblings of the family can also bring this separation by involving themselves too much in the marriage by claiming, "It's our brother!" or "It's our sister!"

This process of leaving and cleaving is not easy when the relationship between the son and his mother is unhealthy. When a son is overly bonded with his mother, he tends not to just become too attached to his mother, he also behaves like a child in the marriage, as he tends to look to his wife for the 'mother figure' he has been used to. This can add to the frustration of the wife, who finds herself having to 'mother' the man while fighting the mother of the man, when she really wants a lover and husband. Such men leave physically but remain attached to their mothers emotionally. Somehow this forces them to depend on their mothers for affirmation and guidance even though they are now married.

The son's continuing dependence on his mother makes her feel needed, so she is reluctant to break this bond. But the result is that there are two women, 'two wombs' contesting for the attention of one man.

The wife, in her effort to win back her husband, may understandably criticise both her husband's dependence and her mother-in-law's interference, which may unfortunately push the man even closer to his mother, because his mother offers affirmation and comfort. In this way, the battle carries on and on.

I once heard a married man proudly claim that he was closer to his mother because blood was thicker than water. The implication here was that because his wife is not a blood relation she could not be trusted as much as his mother. This attitude fuels these insecurities and battles because no wife would want another woman to have an upper hand over her husband. It does not matter if that woman is his mother. The son fails to cleave to his wife as he feels insecure and emasculated by her criticism of his failure to put his mother in her place. The wife also fails to cleave her husband as she is frustrated by the shadow of another woman, in her emotional world. The wife is then forced to fight these shadows alone, as she seeks to bond fully with her husband.

Robert Lewis calls this overbearing mother influence on her son the 'Mom factor', and it cuts deep into a man's psyche, leaving a wound known as the mother wound in his emotions. This overly bonded with mother wound is very subtle; no wonder most men do not even realise it exists. It feels like love, attention and care, but in reality it is control and excessive attention, according to Lewis. That is why the men suffering from it are kind of confused. They do not know how to handle their mother's presence in their marriages. This presence is uncomfortable yet feels sweet, it feels like she is helping. The dilemma is: how does one get rid of something that feels so good? It is more like going against a dentist's advice not to eat sweets to protect your teeth, and this sweet is in your mouth. Do you get to spit it out or just finish it and hope to clean your teeth harder after?

The son's wife can see that her husband is being controlled by his mother but is helpless. This wound is love coated with conditions and reminders of how your mother suffered for you as you were growing up. The emotional implications of this wound are severe and can leave young men paralysed and confused. They want to be with their wives, but the mother's influence and call is so strong that they always gravitate towards the mother. It's a form of colonisation that indebts you to the "aid" your mother gave you as you were growing up. This is a strong emotional umbilical cord that needs a metaphorical midwife to break it.

Men affected by it continue to fuel the feud between the wombs as they feel powerless to face the elephant in the room in their marriage. The problem requires rehabilitation and retraining through vigorous mentoring.

The challenge in marriages today is that many women come to the marriage ready. They are trained, mothered and mentored. They attend home preparation events that give them skills and tricks as well as important gadgets to set them off in their new homes. Men are different! A lot of them are not mentored. May have not been properly fathered or had no father in the home at all, and so have no clue what a father is like. Most of their stag parties are about drinking, jokes and fun. There is no teaching whatsoever about merging with their future spouse. They approach the marriage like a game or fun event and suddenly they realise that they should be heading this new union. Faced with this new responsibility that they are not used to handling, when trouble hits the marriage, they run to their mother.

Every man needs to become independent of his mother for this problem to be resolved. This takes courage, wisdom and understanding in every young man who wants to enjoy a happy, effective, fulfilling, and lasting marriage. This, however, does not come easy!

Jesus mastered this principle early – at the age of twelve, in fact. In LUKE 2:42-49, Mary and Joseph were looking for Jesus after a family visit to Jerusalem. They were on their way back with their extended family when they realised he was not with them. They began a search, but it took three days to find him. They were astonished to find him teaching in the Temple. Mary asked: *"Son, why have you treated us like this? Your father and I have been anxiously searching for you."*

It is worth pointing out that in Jewish tradition at the time, Joseph is the one who should have challenged his son in public, but it is Mary who speaks out first. Undoubtedly, Mary had a strong emotional link with Jesus. This is understandable, as he was not only her son but a miracle son! However, Jesus' answer is my focus in explaining how to break a husband's unhealthy attachment to his mother.

Jesus says: *"Why did you look for me? Did you not know that I am about my Father's business?"* This implied that he was now a man enough to do what his heavenly Father wanted, without their interference. How many of us would be so assertive at 12?! But perhaps only Jesus had a right to say such a thing, as only he was the Son of God as well as the child of Mary.

It seems ungrateful and inconsiderate towards his naturally distressed mother, but let's remember that early rabbinic sources specify 13 as the age at which a boy becomes a legal adult in Jewish culture. So for someone who is also the Son of God, 12 is not such an early age to be thinking of independence!

That said, Jesus was not rebellious towards his parents, and there must have been a quick reconciliation, because we find in the following verse that *"he went down to Nazareth with them and was obedient to them"*.

For Mary, this incident would have felt like a big knife cutting through the emotional bond that she had had with Jesus since his birth. But there comes a point where every son has to 'cut the apron strings' if he is to become a mature adult. Asserting your independence as a man is necessary, and the only safe and effective way to ensure the success of a future marriage. In Jesus' case, he wouldn't be getting married, but in a sense, after this incident, it was now clear that he was 'married' to his mission as the Messiah.

Jesus made it clear that his relationship with his parents had changed. This is what most men need to learn to do in order to stop the battle of the wombs.

Let's look at another example of where Jesus asserts his independence from his mother. In JOHN 2:1-4, Mary came to Jesus and told him that the people had no wine at the wedding. Jesus' response was, *"Woman, why do you involve me? ... My hour has not yet come."* Again, Jesus makes it clear to his mother that his mission takes priority over her wishes. Many young men these days would struggle to address their mothers the way Jesus did. I would not even think of addressing my mother as 'Woman'! It would be considered disrespectful. But when the emotional cord needs to be broken, there is no painless way to do it. It has to be cut, chop! But note that, once he has made it clear that his mother cannot tell him what to do, Jesus' kindness takes over. He turns the water into wine, pleasing his mother and the wedding guests, and helping the host of the feast avoid embarrassment.

Jesus was well aware that his mission was his priority. And if we look on marriage as the mission of a couple who are married, then the marriage has to take priority over other relationships. That is why Jesus affirmed that a couple should not allow anyone to split them apart – which includes mothers-in-law! If the couple fail to put each other first in their marriage, their mission fails. When marriage fails, it is the couple who fail. They cannot ascribe or apportion blame to an outsider! It is their fault if they allow someone else to ruin their marriage.

In yet another account, in MATTHEW 12:46-50, Jesus is speaking to a crowd when his mother and brothers show up and want to speak to him. When he is told of this, Jesus does not stop what he is doing to run to his mother, but again makes it clear that his mission has to take priority over his extended family. He says: *"Who is my mother, and who are my brothers?"* He then points to the disciples and says: *"Here are my mother and my brothers."* This seems harsh – but he is using the incident to make the point that Jesus is making a new family – a family of believers. He explains: *"For whoever does the will of my Father in heaven is my brother and sister and mother."*

Jesus knew how to detach himself from his physical family in order to accomplish his purpose (and make a teaching point of it at the same time!). The same applies to marriage. Men must know that the important person in the marriage is the woman he is married to and no else must come between them – not even "mother and brothers".

But Jesus knew that if he allowed his family to control his life, there was no way he was going to be able to obey his heavenly Father and fully cleave to the people he was sent to – his followers. According to **REVELATION 19:7**, his Church is his bride. Such is the boldness and courage required in every groom to protect his wife from his family.

This does not at all suggest that a man should abandon his family, as Jesus showed us even while dying on the cross. In **JOHN 19:25-27**, as he was about to die, having joined fully to his wife, the Church, he could now minister to his mother through his new spiritual family. He said to Mary: *"'Woman, here is your son,' and to the disciple, 'Here is your mother.' From that time on, this disciple took her into his home."*

Mary gained a son through Jesus and his marriage to the Church. If Jesus had not taken time to develop a good relationship with his disciples, Mary would not have had another son. If Jesus had not taken time to cleave to his bride when Mary and her family tried to pull him away when he was teaching the crowd (**MATTHEW 12:46-50**), Mary would have not had another son to take care of her after the death of Jesus.

This is the purpose of marriage, to broaden our families by adding new sons and daughters to us for growth and development. The challenge for many men in their marriages today is to remove their emotional dependence on their mothers in order to properly cleave to their wives.

A child is attached to its mother in the womb for nine months. At birth they are separated, by the cutting of the umbilical cord. If this separation does not happen, infections that can lead to the death of either person could occur. This physical separation is usually easy because it is done by the midwives or doctors who deliver the baby. The emotional attachment is different and continues for a long time, as the child depends on its mother for survival and development.

Because of this, the mother's bond is strong. This attachment is even stronger where a son is brought up by a single mother, as it is focused only on the mother, as there is no father around to depend upon. As a boy grows, he must gradually learn independence, as we have seen in Jesus's case.

Where this independence has not happened, there needs to be a metaphorical midwife who can safely cut off the emotional 'umbilical cord'. Most cultures lack these skilled people – although good marriage counsellors do exist in some societies. Some cultures conduct coming-of-age ceremonies that mark a point where boys become men, linking them up with older men in the community, who then mentor the boys, preparing them for manhood and fatherhood. This can be very helpful.

In my culture, the boys looked after cattle and goats during the day, whilst the girls spent their time with mothers in the home being taught and groomed in the way of women. This helped with this emotional separation over time. Boys also developed a sense of being men, as they did things that were considered 'manly'. We were taught hunting, fighting and defending ourselves, looking after animals and learning the chores that men in the village did. This helped us identify with men and learn how to handle women and other situations that needed a man. Boys with absent or distant fathers or broken communities lacked this important phase of their lives. They tended to be more attached to their mothers and their mothers did not quite know how to release them when they were of age.

In the politically correct society of developed countries like Britain, the gender fluid ideology that has grown up makes it even more difficult for men to understand their male identity and their role in marriage.

CHAPTER TWO

THE RIGHT WAY

I view the mother-in-law and daughter-in-law relationship as parallel lines that can flow together without overlapping. Each should have its own space. Then the relationship can be productive and joyful.

The story of Mary being taken care of by one of the disciples (John) after the death of Jesus is a good example of how Christian relationships should empower us by broadening our families. A Catalonian proverb says, "A mother-in-law may be good but she is better when mother earth covers her up." This is the wrong way of viewing this beautiful relationship, as it is a description of the relationship when it is dysfunctional. I do not think that is how John and Mary viewed their relationship as they left the foot of the cross for home that day. Jesus was specific on how they were to relate in future – as mother and son! The Catalonian proverb is a typical example of helplessness, bitterness and pain. Mothers-in-law are good and beneficial when they do not dominate their son. They can be a blessing and great support to a marriage.

Christians should introduce new proverbs of hope and understanding if we are to change these terrible attitudes in our society. The Japanese have also had their take on this sensitive relationship. "Never glory on the morning or smiles of your mother-in-law," they say. Again, this is the opinion of a person who had a torrid time with their mother-in-law. Who wants the world to be interpreted from their painful experience? There are mothers-in-law whose smile comes from a clean and a pure heart, that sees a daughter or a son as Jesus taught the crowds at the foot of the cross. The truth is that not all mothers-in-law have this problem. Those of us with good mothers-in-law and good daughters-in-law should start speaking well about them in order to counter the negative proverbs about this special relationship. My mother has an amazing relationship with my wife.

I heard of a mother-in-law who went to fetch her son's daughter and enrolled her at a school closer to herself without the consent of her daughter-in-law. This is a clear indication of the foolishness of a mother-in-law who has been given too much power by her son. Her reason for doing this was that she wanted to enjoy her grandchild. This was an inconsiderate way to approach this aspect of life. The mother would also want to enjoy her own child, and has more right to do so. Such are the experiences that cause certain women to hate and fight their mothers-in-law.

Couples need to be vigilant about relationships with in-laws. What may seem fine now may not be soon, if ground is given to them.

I will not end this line of thought before considering the Spanish who say, "Well married is when you have no mother-in-law and no sister-in-law." This critical attitude, as we have seen, is a global phenomenon caused by an unhealthy closeness between a son and his mother.

I know of a mother-in-law who physically beat her daughter-in-law. Another mother-in-law confronted her son after he bought his wife a new car. Her reason was that the son had never bought his mother a car, even though she had worked hard and sacrificed a lot to bring him up. There is another story of a mother-in-law who demanded to join the newlyweds on their honeymoon – and the son bought her the ticket! This is not the way to handle the mother-son relationship if his marriage is to be successful!

CHAPTER THREE

THE CHALLENGE

Every married family belongs to three different families, each of which may have different political persuasions, moral standards and beliefs about bringing up children. These different opinions can contribute to the feuds and battles between mothers and their daughters-in-law.

Carl von Clausewitz once said, "Politics is the womb in which war develops." We see political wars across the world, and some of them over very small differences, resulting in huge loss of life and gross destruction of property and infrastructure. George Bush's Iraq War is a good example. Saddam Hussein had not attacked America but was accused of possessing weapons of mass destruction and harbouring terrorists. Saddam's regime was cruel to his own people, and on previous form (Iraq's invasion of Kuwait which triggered the first Gulf War) it was a potential danger to the world, but the war began on the basis of faulty or flimsy intelligence – or some say outright lies. The Americans announced victory over Baghdad, Saddam's statues were toppled and there was dancing and celebration in the streets. They thought it was all over. Winning the war had been relatively easy; winning the peace afterwards proved anything but.

It's similar sometimes when marriages break down. It begins with gossip and false rumours, which turn into all out 'war'. One partner wins the divorce case in court, hoping that is the end of the problem. But it is over twenty years since the Iraq War now and those weapons of mass destruction have not been discovered, but the damage, havoc and repercussions caused are still being felt till this day. It is little different after a sour divorce. Custody battles continue, bitterness and disputes continue, and the children feel like pawns in a parental power game. The distress and anguish can not only ruin the subsequent lives of the divorcees but even more so of their children.

The power struggle of a mother and daughter-in-law's relationship – the battle of the wombs – can be as destructive to family life as political power struggles are between nations. The mother-in-law who hasn't let her son go feels she still has a right over her son. The daughter-in-law is made to feel like she married his mother, yet in her vows she is joined to her husband. This should be her time to establish herself as the new mother in preparation for her womb to bring forth, perpetuating the cycle the Almighty set in motion in the Garden of Eden when he said, *"Be fruitful and multiply. Fill the earth and govern it"* (**Genesis 1:28, NLT**).

Duval (1954) commented about this battle and suggested that "the young couple requires autonomy in order to develop an independent family unit". This does not always happen, resulting in the fierce battle of the wombs. Literature by Kieren, Henton and Maotz (1975) revealed that in most cases of marital conflict, both husbands and wives believe that the husband's relatives are frequently the source of the conflict rather than the wife's kin. This has been confirmed from the few cases I have experienced and the stories alluded to in the chapters before.

The Bible is clear that clear separation is the solution to this: *"Therefore shall a man leave his father and his mother, and shall cleave unto his wife"* (**Genesis 2:24, KJV**). The parents should no longer have control over their children. But for some reason the man's family often carries a sense of entitlement, refusing to give room for the daughter-in-law to grow into her role.

This attitude is further exacerbated by some cultures that favour the boy child over the girl child. Here girls are viewed in a lesser light to the boys and more investment is channelled towards empowering the male child. This opens up more opportunities of employment to boys, leaving girls at the mercy of men in marriage. Women then enter marriage as a way of escape from their poverty, at the same time making them subservient in the marriage relationship. Because of this perspective of approaching marriage from a needy platform, the woman is disempowered and wounded in a controlling and crowded marriage. Husbands contribute to this struggle by not protecting their wives, leaving them to fight alone, partly because of this culture.

Another problem is that marriage is a communal thing in certain cultures, where the family of the man makes all decisions with the help of their son. The woman in this case becomes a slave that is there to be supported and bear children for the man. More women than men report difficulty in this area, according to Duval.

It is also confirmed that more female in-laws are found more troublesome than male in-laws, hence the battle of the wombs. In the case of sisters, one wonders whether this is caused by envy from those whose marriages have not gone well, who therefore vent their frustration on their brother's marriage? This is corroborated by Duval (1954), who observed that in-laws tend to be meddlesome, interfering and dominating – and the driving culprit is the mother in-law.

The only way a mother-in-law's interference can be broken is by her son putting her in her place. It sounds harsh, but if done in a sensitive way it is the best thing to do. Unfortunately, many men are afraid to confront their mothers, leaving their wives in this toxic environment. Sadly, a toxic environment makes everything in it toxic, hence the fightback from the daughter-in-law, leading to protracted battles that are punctuated with finger pointing and empty accusations.

CHAPTER FOUR

THE STRONGHOLD

To avoid these battles, the Bible set a path to follow when a new family is inaugurated. Unfortunately, most people do not take the wisdom of the Bible seriously, leading to problems and strife. In **GENESIS 2:24**, God directly instructed Adam and Eve on how to establish new families, as theirs would be the first. They had an understanding, wise and good Parent – who was both their Father and Father-in-law – so it was easy for them. Eve did not have the challenges of a mother-in-law to deal with. She was told what to do in order for peace to prevail between her and her children when they married: *"A man shall leave his father and mother and be joined to his wife, and they shall become one flesh"* (**GENESIS 2:24, NJKV**).

As I have said, Jesus reiterated this important process in **MARK 10:6-8 (NJKV)**: *"But from the beginning of the creation, God 'made them male and female. For this reason a man shall leave his father and mother and be joined to his wife, and the two shall become one flesh'; so then they are no longer two, but one flesh."*

Here is the process. The man must leave his mother and father and be joined to his wife. When mothers-in-law are fighting their daughters-in-law, they are actually fighting the process that God instituted. They are not giving room for their sons to be one with the woman of their choice. Mothers become the stronghold that forms a barrier because they refuse to let go of their sons. Instead, they get into the marriage with their sons! The son may also be complicit in that he may not have the courage to 'flee the nest'. This is particularly strong in the African culture, where young men think they are honouring their parents by not correcting them when they cross the line, even when they are out of order.

As we have seen from the proverbs that mock mother and daughter-in-law relationships across different cultures, our traditions are a huge stronghold. Jesus pointed out the negative impact our traditions can have on our marriages. He bemoaned the human emphasis on the traditions of men at the expense of the Word of God: *"You have let go of the commands of God and are holding on to human traditions"* (**MARK** 7:8). He went on to rebuke the religious leaders: *"You have a fine way of setting aside the commands of God in order to observe your own traditions!"* (verse 9). This crucial observation by Jesus led Paul to warn his congregations about the dangers of men's traditions that conflict with God's Word: *"See to it that no one takes you captive through hollow and deceptive philosophy, which depends on human tradition and the elemental spiritual forces of this world rather than on Christ"* (**COLOSSIANS 2:8**).

The relationship between a husband and wife is a crucial one for society as it is meant to model the relationship between Christ and the Church – his bride. The Apostle Paul says to husbands: *"Love your wives, just as Christ loved the church and gave himself up for her to make her holy…"* (**EPHESIANS 5:25-26**). Here the Bible teaches men how to treat their wives – with the same love and sacrifice that Jesus made for the Church! This is the highest of standards. And why did Christ give his life for us? To make us holy. To make holy means to venerate, to regard with great respect, and to separate out for service to God! This is how wives should be treated by their husbands – with the greatest respect, and separated from her family in order to be of service to her husband, just as the husband gives himself in service to her as much as Christ gave his life up for us!

We have seen what happened when Jesus' family tried to interfere in his marriage to the Church. He made it clear where his priorities lay. LUKE 8:21 puts Jesus' response in these words: *"My mother and brothers are those who hear God's word and put it into practice."* In other words, my family is now my followers who obey God. As Christ's followers are his bride, then we can paraphrase this as: "My wife is the one I am married to and she has pre-eminence in my life!" Many traditions have gone against this godly principle, creating their own traditions that demean the wife and treat her like an outsider, an insignificant person in the marriage relationship.

It is the responsibility of the man to protect his wife, give her confidence and the space she needs to grow and develop as a wife and mother. The two shall become one! A divided house will not stand.

I came to realise this very early in my marriage. I saw that I needed to protect my wife because when she came to my family, she was from a totally different culture and background. My family was used to me and worked with me. Many times my wife was treated as though she did not exist, not intentionally, but because they were not used to her. They found it easier to approach and deal with me by default. This caused her to struggle, as she felt side-lined as a wife. My mother, my sisters and everyone else was happy except her. I had to come to her rescue by teaching them how to work with me through her. In the end, none of my family members were allowed to come directly to me with their requests. They had to come through my wife. It was hard at first, but they quickly learned as we put our foot down. She was now in charge of my life.

The process of becoming one is a long and precarious one that needs understanding, maturity and boldness, as well as humility and a teachable spirit.

A revelation came to me that my mother was my father's wife and she came into the Sibanda household by marriage to my father. Equally, Fatima was my wife and she had come into the Sibanda household through her marriage to me. That made them sisters! They are equal and should operate as parallel lines within this household. From then on, I could challenge the tradition that argued that my wife was inferior to my mother. I taught my mother to go through my wife each time she needed something from me. My mother taught my family the same. The result was a healthy relationship, where each person operates in their space with the respect they deserve. This has brought joy, peace, growth, and fulfilment in our family.

I believe we have a functioning marriage that has lasted 29 years mainly because of tackling the position of my wife in my marriage and her relationship with my family. A lot of young men cannot do that, and they have paid dearly in their marital relationships. They are still tied down to traditions they do not even understand, encouraging an unnecessary battle to fester and continue. This stronghold needs to be broken, so that "the two shall become one."

CHAPTER FIVE

THE BATTLE OF THE WOMBS

I learnt this early in my marriage when there was an issue in the family. I was not one of those boys who never grew up with my father, but I didn't see much of him. He was away at work and we remained in the township with my mother. I had more of my mother's influence than my father's. I only saw my father for about seven days during the Christmas holidays. My mother's DNA is in my psyche and sometimes that can go deep! As my mother was making a point one day, I found myself having to make a choice between my mother and my wife.

The choice was clear in my heart, although very hard to verbalise. With her eyes wide open, my mother declared, "Osien is my son! He slept in this womb for nine months. I carried him for nine months and no one can tell me what to say about my son!" Here is the politics of the womb! A chill went down my spine, as my mother was not seeing the new context that was evolving. There was something she was missing, even though she was right in what she was saying. The problem was that this was no longer relevant for where we were and where we were going. I was now a man and now thinking like a man, as Paul noted in one of his writings. I had to become that man by coming to my wife's defence and support. It was uncomfortable, it was not easy, but that was the way for me to have a confident wife and a stable marriage.

When my daughter was still very small, I quickly realised that while I slept in my mother's womb for nine months, it had taken another womb to make me a father that I was now so proud to be. I knew at that point that I did not need to be the third force in this battle. If I played my cards well, the rightful womb would be assured of victory. This is the exchange zone, where most relay teams lose the race if the baton is not passed smoothly. If not done properly, the battle of the wombs ensues. Most men fail at this point, and the battle gets protracted for a long time, hurting relationships and breaking marriages in the process.

My mother worked very hard for us, I admit. She was a diligent woman who I admire deeply and passionately. She is the strategist that made us the success we are today, but that has its place. Here is the point: my mother was right that she is my mother. My wife cannot be my mother. That is uncontested. My mother had the honour of bringing me into this world and that cannot be taken from her. It has its place; it had its season. I quickly realised that my wife had her own womb, that ran parallel to my mother's. I was the right person to comment on that in order to mediate this battle. One was past and the other was current.

This brings together Jesus' analogy of the comparison between new wine skins and the old wine skins battling to contain the new wine! *"No one pours new wine into old wineskins. Otherwise, the new wine will burst the skins; the wine will run out and the wineskins will be ruined. No, new wine must be poured into new wineskins. And no one after drinking old wine wants the new, for they say, 'The old is better'"* (LUKE 5:37-39). Jesus was right!

Having gone through the motions in my mind, I appreciated my mother for being my mother. I assured her that the owner and record of being my mother belonged to her, and no one could ever challenge her on that. I went on further to point out that given a choice, I would not want to go back into her womb. I also said that I would rather sleep in my wife's arms rather than try to squeeze myself in her womb. That is where I find peace and solace. I made my mother understand that both their wombs are valuable to me, but each has a season and now the important womb for the season I was in was that of my wife. One was a new wine skin and the other an old one with different experiences that will never appeal to the new skin.

My mother and my wife were equal in their entry into the Sibanda household. My father brought her in through marriage. I did the same for my wife. Their wombs are parallel lines that must maintain their honour without interfering with the other. My mother cannot enjoy the benefits of being my father's wife as well as the benefits that my wife should have. She needs to give my wife space without trying to make her do things her way.

After the point was made, there was a moment of silence and deep gasps of air that led to a change of heart. That was the beginning of a new dawn, where my wife was accepted as a mother in the family as well. She has even gone further to assume the role of my mother when there are family events. The baton is now safely in her hand to take it to the finish line. The family has benefited in the process. This is how the battle was stopped in my family. I say again, some men fail to take this road in order to protect their wives and they pay dearly for this failure.

I once conducted a marriage seminar where this was a hot topic. The men were adamant that their mothers were more important than their wives because they gave birth to them. While this may make cultural sense, it is spiritually devoid of principle. Birds have a good way of managing the nest syndrome. When the time comes for birds to fly from the nest, they never go back there again. They leave and cleave, literally. Birds do not even visit the nest they grew up in. They embrace the new and forget about an old nest that will not help them in future. The battle of the womb occurs where sons are still clinging onto the nest, or mothers fail to evict them.

It is understandable that our mothers will feel a sense of loss when we get married. That is the process of procreation. My wife needs the space and the support to be the new mother without interference, and many African cultures fail in that regard.

Earlier I mentioned the story of a mother-in-law who demanded to go on honeymoon with her son and his new bride after their wedding. This was a wounded woman who could not release her son. Instead of seeing her daughter-in-law as a blessing, who had come to give her grandchildren, she saw her as a competitor who had come to take her son away. She was now trying to make the new wife uncomfortable by her presence. The son failed to be the protector of his wife in the process and allowed his mother to be the poison in his marriage.

I have learnt to protect my wife and give her the cover she needs for her to do well among my family members. Our marriage has been enriched by that understanding and approach. Mothers who interfere in their son's marriages still have a marriage to go back to. Sons who fail to correct this will not have a marriage to go back to when the mother returns to her own. This behaviour is a sign of a wound in one's soul. Wounds are caused by deeper problems that were never confronted in time, until they formed ugly scars that are difficult to remove.

I recently heard of a mother-in-law who had left her husband and moved in with her newly married son in a different country. She moved into their home for a long period of time and has now become a citizen. The son has not challenged his mother, yet she continues to frustrate his wife. Our men must be taught to deal with this battle otherwise their marriages will suffer.

CHAPTER SIX

IS THERE A MODEL?

The Bible has two clear references where a mother-in-law is mentioned in a marital relationship or home environment. The first is Peter's mother-in-law, who happened to be sick in Peter's house in **Matthew 8:14-15**. This portion of scripture says nothing directly about the relationship between Peter and his mother-in-law, but the fact that his mother-in-law was being cared for in his home suggests that he may have had a good relationship with her.

The book of Ruth, however, sheds some light and great deal of encouragement on this subject. Ruth and Naomi had an amazing relationship that every mother-in-law and daughter-in-law would envy. It is highly possible to have a good relationship between these two unique wombs. One might argue that the reason that their relationship was good was because the third force, Ruth's husband and Naomi's son, does not exist at this stage of the relationship. He had died long before. That may be true but there is much more to the story.

I believe the relationship between in-laws should improve over time, just as the marriage should. It is said, "There is no privacy between a husband and wife, not when mommy is in the middle." But if 'mommy' is not interfering, and "the son is in the middle", respecting his mother but prioritising his wife, then there should be a healthy relationship between husband and wife, and wife and mother-in-law.

In fact, Ruth and Naomi destroy every negative argument and instead assert that it is very possible to have a good relationship between mother-in-law and daughter-in-law. They are the ultimate role models!

Ruth says to Naomi: *"Where you go I will go, and where you stay I will stay. Your people will be my people and your God my God. Where you die I will die, and there I will be buried"* (**RUTH 1:16-17**). This is not a statement that comes from a daughter-in-law who has had a nasty experience with her mother-in-law! Signs suggest that this relationship was healthy and functional long before Ruth's husband died. No woman in her right mind could commit to following an evil mother-in-law to a land where she has no support from a loving family. I would argue that Naomi was the ultimate mother-in-law. This made Ruth the ultimate daughter-in-law, and their relationship the ultimate mother/daughter-in-law relationship.

Ruth's words to Naomi are a deep spiritual sentiment that is pregnant with trust, confidence, peace, total surrender, and an emotional attachment. Ruth was so confident in her relationship with Naomi that she was ready to leave her home country and her own parents and cleave to Naomi. Her vow to Naomi was so strong that it was similar to a marriage covenant. She clearly loved her very much.

I believe that it was similar with Peter's mother-in-law in Matthew 8, because she was happy to be nursed in Peter's house in her time of vulnerability and need, until Jesus came to heal her.

The key to such a good relationship is godliness and understanding your space and margins. I am convinced this is possible because I witnessed this first-hand in my own home. My wife and my mother are a 'Ruth and Naomi' of their own kind, though they have not experienced the pain and desperation of Moab and Bethlehem. They love each other, laugh together, and have a lot of fun together. My wife literally looks after my mother. She provides her with all that she needs. She even has a pension and a set pay day for her; and I am still alive!

IS THERE A MODEL?

My wife's entire family love my mother and they look after her as well. My brother-in-law visits my mother when he travels to Africa. The relationship goes beyond my wife. My mother loves them too, because she does not view them as a people that came to take away her son. Instead, she sees the value they have added, not only to me but our entire family as well.

Other than the practical witness I have had in my own home, the other critical ingredient in the success of Naomi and Ruth's relationship is the God factor. Ruth introduces this in her commitment: "Your God shall be my God." Many of us have recited Ruth's words for our wedding vows yet our relationships turn sour. The question is why? Ruth was a godly woman, and so was Naomi. The fear of God is the wisdom that we need to live well with one another, and the key to solving battles. My belief is that Ruth and Naomi were very close before Naomi's husband and sons died.

CHAPTER SEVEN

THE IDEAL RELATIONSHIP

Jesus raised an important point that I find is a problem in many relationships. *"These people honour me with their lips, but their hearts are far from me"* (**MATTHEW 15:8**). We tend to be quick to offer lip service that we rarely back with our actions. In contrast, Ruth meant what she said and expressed it in the actions she took, even in difficult circumstances.

First, Ruth honoured and served her mother-in-law with all of her heart. We see her asking Naomi's permission to go and work: *"Let me go to the fields and pick up the leftover grain…"* (**RUTH 2:2**). She understood her place and how to relate to her mother-in-law with respect, though she was stronger and free to do as she desired. Respect will take a person far in their relationship with their in-laws.

Naomi responded very affectionately to Ruth's request: *"Go ahead, my daughter."* This is not a false relationship. Boaz confirms this good relationship: *"I've been told all about what you have done for your mother-in-law since the death of your husband – how you left your father and mother and your homeland and came to live with a people you did not know before"* (**RUTH 2:11**). The principle of leaving and cleaving is clearly demonstrated in Ruth's attitude to her marriage. She left her father and mother and became committed to the family of her husband, Mahlon.

This is the kind of commitment that Jesus taught us at the foot of the cross as he said to Mary, *"Woman, here is your son"*, and to the disciple, *"Here is your mother"* (JOHN 19:26-27). This concept must be understood, believed and applied for marriages to last. Ruth was godly and followed the Word of God with her heart. She was not emotionally attached to her people. She learned to separate herself by leaving and cleaving to Mahlon and his people and his God, as the Bible teaches.

Many of us are so overly bonded with our families, that we bring them into our marriages. We should of course love our own families, but not allow such ties to take precedent over our marriages.

There was once an incident with one of my friends, who had a difficult time with her sister-in-law. She was staying with them and made sure that she got between my friend and her husband. The sister-in-law felt such a sense of entitlement to the point that she would use the shower room attached to their bedroom, even though there was a common bathroom downstairs. Her husband did nothing about it. In the same scenario, the sister-in-law changed the kitchen colour scheme without consulting the wife of the house. Her argument when challenged was, "This is my brother's house." Imagine what would have happened if the man had died. Do you think his wife would say to the sister-in-law, "Where you go, I will go"?! She would show her sister-in-law the door as soon as the funeral was over!

Another of my friends lost her husband many years ago in South Africa. The man's family came to mourn and bury their son. Before the funeral, the in-laws had already taken the car keys, threatening to take their son's car. The car was bought on hire purchase had not been fully paid off. Instead of them allowing the woman to mourn her husband, she now had to contend with hostile in-laws who were bent on taking advantage of her vulnerable state. I had to take the car and hide it at my house until they left. It caused a big fight that ended up involving the police. It was very embarrassing, but I had now learnt how to deal with difficult in-laws, so I protected her. Ruth did not experience this pain when her husband died, as the Book of Ruth shows us.

As Ruth was gleaning in the hot sun, she was offered some food (2:14). She ate and kept back some for her mother-in-law who had remained at home. When she returned, she gave Naomi the food that she had kept for her. This is a genuine mother/daughter relationship, deeply rooted in love.

There is a dramatic change of events in chapter 3, where Naomi sets up Ruth to be married by Boaz. This was a huge sacrifice for Naomi, because according to the tradition of the culture, Boaz was supposed to marry Naomi! But she knew that her womb was no longer fertile. Earlier she'd asked Ruth and Orpah rhetorically: *"Am I going to have any more sons, who could become your husbands?"* (1:11). The answer was obvious. Her womb had run its course, and it was time for her to support a womb with "fresh legs" in order to fulfil her destiny.

Naomi was not threatened my Ruth's womb. She was ready to support and mentor her, even if it meant that Ruth would marry the man Naomi was entitled to marry. Many a mother-in-law would never have accepted that! When Ruth conceived, the women of Israel celebrated with Naomi and said, *"'Praise the Lord, who has now provided a redeemer for your family! May this child be famous in Israel. May he restore your youth and care for you in your old age. For he is the son of your daughter-in-law who loves you and has been better to you than seven sons!'"* (4:14-15, **NLT**).

Naomi responded by caring for the baby as if he were her own. This is a definitive example of a good mother/daughter-in-law relationship. Naomi now had a family to spend time with and who would look after her in her old age, after losing both her sons and her husband. Who is able to achieve this? Only a woman who fears the Lord.

OTHER BOOKS BY SIBANDA PUBLISHING

Books by Osien Sibanda

The Value of Kindness

The Principles and Practice of Giving

The God Told Me Syndrome

Count the Cost

The Pursuit of God: 30 Day Devotional

The Miracles of Jesus: 30 Day Devotional

The Parables of Jesus: 30 Day Devotional

Great Prayers by Great People: 30 Day Devotional

The Way to Great Faith

The Heart of An Ant

OTHER BOOKS BY SIBANDA PUBLISHING

Books by Fatima Sibanda

The Fragrance of a Godly Woman

Daughter Arise!
*Defy Your Limitations and
Scale the Utmost Height*

Your Path is Becoming Brighter

You Can Do a Beautiful Thing

Diligence: *Pathway to Destiny*

For more information please contact
info@sibandapublishing.com

www.ingramcontent.com/pod-product-compliance
Lightning Source LLC
Chambersburg PA
CBHW050450010526
44118CB00013B/1761